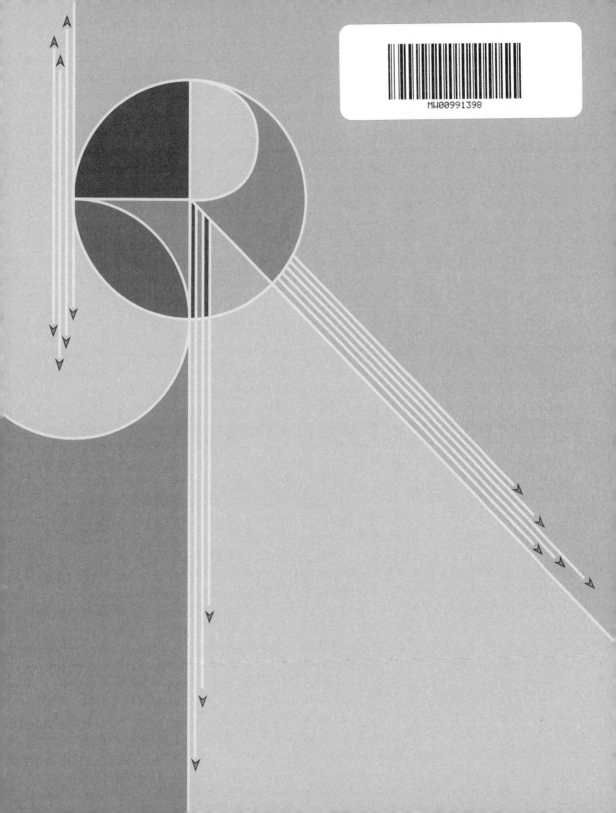

THESE ARE THE
GLORIA STORIES

Published by Factory Hollow Press
a Division of Flying Object

Flying Object Center
for Independent Publishing
Art, & the Book, Inc.

Factory Hollow Press c/o Flying Object
42 West Street, Hadley, MA 01035

flying-object.org • factoryhollowpress.com

ISBN: 978-0-9835203-4-4
First edition

Factory Hollow Press titles are distributed to the trade by
Small Press Distribution • spdbooks.org

Front cover illustration by Mary Austin Speaker

Designed by Flying Object
Printed by McNaughton & Gunn

Flying Object is 501(c)(3) nonprofit art and publishing organization.

These Are The Gloria Stories

Kelin Loe

Factory Hollow Press
Hadley, MA

For my teachers.

Hearts of oak, did you go down

Kirkê asked

Biochemically, I am more alive
than you

and when
the kitchen light cuts

out I become
more to you

I mean I can candle

when I find
an almost-dead
finch I am next to
it, what
happens next.

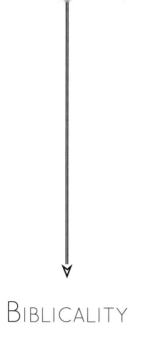

BIBLICALITY

GO GO GREEN HELL—I'm all groan—I'm all grown up—

We waited and blasted pragmatic and frantic past the immaculate break in the latex, patty cake in our gas tank, the alchemy elastic of our fastening Cadillac evaporated after this fucking jocular massacre.

The butane baby will blame us later—gain our better taint. Terrained and aged and awful and screw the grater so so bad—

Awake in the hallway—I'm not scattered about you—I'm all about you—

Agree with mediocrity—at some point you leave so banner your hands on me. Borrow these bed sheets and battle the breaking babel with wound.

I see your pee and know it's noon and I haven't peed today. Chase this tang chase this pain chase this exacting tang and manipulating parade after forsaking your other alter-eager as I scuffle through each and every year tell me ten more times do you want me here.

I was made to believe there's something wrong with me—sorry this noise is all my honesty.

The tapping nails on this ultimatum matchboard watch me playing Mary. Take anticipation like a bulb in the armpit, mistake in the bulgur.

Poon like it's over me. I know your voice isn't this deep (it works for me).

Family pulping. It smells like the in between of a tree's ass cheeks in here. Pardon practically and spatter. This gets worse worse.

Lock this in lock this in. I'm worried I will let this down. Don't let up—let the cartography get the rest of you—don't let eternity make this lonely.

I smell chiefly trees between you—this is a mess of matter timber—thicket equipment greater than every dick in this slitting perpendicular splayed and delaying static—polaris and kited pudendum—onerous precise and terrified—that's about the size of it.

Futurecome futurecome collapse in collecting all these extra. I could spread them out again. I'm asking after your ascot. I can't neck my way to you, it's time I came for you.

Go, go, green ghosts! Meet our melody loaded home! The entry is way way eager. Greet this slow and siren.

The Boxer

for Staff Sergeant Christopher McGurk

clydesdales , hot dogs and dollar shots — meet me here OR no oven mitts on fire in here ! ! !

i will make these lasagnas in 15 minutes wearing nothing but those panties !

tracing my umbrella now. how the rib meets the rod is unclear .

penises hanging everywhere and nobody's worried but me   !

somebody please quit making out in the library it sounds like eating stew !! and please tell me if i need to poop or otherwise —

been eating cereal like its meal so much corn and so much time to eat the corn and grind grind and i believe you followed the trail of sugar to find me yesterday so

HERE I   AM , HONEY POT ! ! !

i keep opening the internet like there is food in there .

before my husband was my husband i learned that men don't wipe after number one .

and, as an aviator , how do you feel about my relationship with my husband ? ??

can you or can you not see it ? ?

please is it made of MATTER HOW much can it mean ? ?

banana bag ! NOW !! and a middle-aged man to tell me FACTS .

better stay at home and launder the carpet over and over ... PARDON you believe in me
right ??

i was the one who borrowed your dollars

i was the one who blanked on your name because I HAVE THE POWER to BLANK

i'll move across your room like livestock in the light

I WILL GROW MY HAIR UNTIL IT IS LONGER THAN MYTH !!! ! !

largely i haven't happened .

largely you haven't lately you and i have . ...

i spitted you out you spitted me down .

time to wash me out of your hair and stand up .

IF we insist on leaving the house , THEN we will be OUT IN battle ! !! !

fuck my concentration — when i imagine FIGHT i am all PLOW and no PUNCH .

when i take you DOWN — i am all defensive end kicked out of the profession and operating without MODERATION above the astroturf , braced and rushing — i am ossified from eyes to spine —

let me see you thinking of me .

you will not think of me without me watching you .

YES, i have a bronze erection . and YES it really hurts thanks .

i learned erections can hurt from my husband — also i learned testicles are not handles !!!

mostly i am talking , mostly to my husband but this is not for my husband because if i had something to tell him   , i would just tell him , RIGHT ? ?   ?

i've been gone a lot at night   . TELL ME is my absence a GAP or a HOLE or a STILL or a problem ? ?

i've been nesting with village idiots . three important things to note: ONE we are tidy TWO we have more fight than a virus THREE we have more anger than implied in vengeance !!

i'm sorry —   are you AWARE of my condition ?

do you UNDERSTAND what it means to have me in the room ? ?   ? do you know what that means for you ?

CONSIDER ME : i have been a gentleman   .

TELL ME : my friends know that   ? ?   ?   ?

my goal for you is to HERE a BELL — follow the DUEL meaning of DONG

as in i love favorites together like having our wedding day every day but i love the smell of gasoline and i love the smell of fennel SO :   how to mix those ?

YOU HAVEN'T PAID ATTENTION   .

every wet entrance to the body is a TELL .

UNITL you LEARN to LISTEN to LIGHT ,

i'll be at the back of your every orgasm

WAVING   !!! ! ! !

where is my sniper ? ?

and just how many shits does it take to get your attention ? ? been hand washing rabbits this afternoon THUS do you think the rabbits are dead or alive ?? in a basin or a pot ??

i know what i'm getting for christmas — all the sex i forgot about this year already . i get roped into a lot of things WE NEED ANOTHER HOT GLUE GUN AGAIN sorry

hunk of fur in my fist — thick — can you catch this ?

ALMIGHTY ANIMAL , RAISE YOUR WIGGLING NOSE TO THE SKY !!

don't worry about the lights —

you will look where i tell you to look .

did you know i'm from minnesota ? my husband is too . there used to be an ice palace in st paul every january lit up in pink and blue .

if you TRY TO SLOW me DOWN i will FRACTURE your comprehension of CHILL though i don't want to .

COLD is NOT a NUMB BULGE IT IS A STILLNESS —

somedays the only way to chase it is to finalize yourself .

if i die young   , will you EXPLAIN it and TAKE CARE of it ?

will you take care of your self ? ??

i'm pretty sure i'm alive because f scott fitzgerald died

and when i survive i will be the fight landed .

you DESERVE so much more from ME than this wrangle .

i will pay in pluck and brass and rattle .

i want you to make it   !

and when you do , i want you to act humble .

Good Manners

We'd made this huge mess. And the people in the street began to cheer!

Like they'd never seen a landmine before.

I guess folks around here don't see too many landmines.

They don't see too many pockets either.

Are you talking about grenades?

How do you get someone to keep something without telling them to keep it, anyway?

I just found your ring in the shower.

The water's back?

I've never been so good at talking with my eyes.

We had these eyestalks.

They were taller than antlers. I can tell you what we saw.

You probably couldn't see yourself.

We wouldn't have wanted to!

The eyes—they don't get wet!

And at that point, we really wanted a bath.

I've needed a bath.

Really??? I can help.

Loving anyone in the summer is excessive. Everything is already touching you.

We didn't ever run into any summers.

He means matters.

But did they touch you?

In that neck is like a Lincoln Log.

Often it felt like scruffing it.

Are you hungry?
In a very old way.

We saw a lot of hair.

Mostly on bodies.

Still, it was usually the cause of my coughing.

Didn't you bring packing tape?

Wouldn't have mattered with all the scabs.

We had to use all the tape on the ashtrays anyway.

So your mother found you.

It's more like we found a lot of ants.

Ants and cows.

You are an iconic place for a band-aid.
I put my best boob forward.
I could go for a breast blitz.
You could only bow to it.
I was promised a kingdom.
What about the edge of my boat neck?
And all I got was a center part.

They were content to believe that my farts were the dog's.

Kibble refers to everything he shat on.

You mistook the tracks for the truck.

He mistook the ladle for her hand.

The land was something you never understood.

At least I had my hands free.

I told you to never trust silence in the bathroom.
I told you not to check.

You can notch another brawl into your belt.
You should see the other bride.
Bet she dropped like a sack of hair.
Bet she broke like a bean.
I fell an elk that day.
You were married?

I crunched my ear in my sleep last night.
Yes! I was walking down your precious street!
I presume you saw the bricks.
Did you see me?
No one intended anything by you.

I like to perform but that has nothing to do with this.

You never did come up clapping.

You asked me for so much more than my arms.

Go ahead.

I asked you because I have good manners.

THE MOTORIST

Breathe this   air here from my stomach.   Breathe this air here   I have plenty.
Breathe this air   here is the point   we've all been in after—   that is either
a dead little toad   or a wrapper.   That is either an egg flower
or look what the poor do for attention.

We've eaten strap after   the crabapple, parented   the eggplant, changed
the barometer to record   the rate of the lobotomy   hammer. Beelzebub and
Abigail are engaged to   be married. If you're going
to be back in town,   I will need you to place
your hands on the bar.

I routed over the onion elk,   kaleidoscoped   the spit. Sip   with me   now. And after all you eat   I am the mammoth.   And I am after   your apple puppets.

Pipe dreams! Parade   the membranes   and pig tails. Watch   for little   fingers. Grass over the water   germander. You are   not supposed to look   me in the eye.

These cups   cover your ears.   If you   aren't here   then leave.

Shovel them   bones! Beelzebub   never   asked. You   mean   I have to   go somewhere   to wash   my clothes?

I have had the flixweed   under your gums. I have   had you ever   after the
gum the greater   value of   the dawn over   the garden   as seen from my
shoulder   have you ever   after the   hail. I am   the better man!

I've missed you I   know after what afghan   I can't but   Abigail will
have daffodils that   remember   the afghan is   a warm knot.

Lately urine rises   like a   knife. The cotton   dust of your sanitary
napkins settled in   your nail beds.   A sigh, a second
after. Abby   told me.

Been keeping   the bryony   happy. After   that I never   strolled any
more. Then I   bet our nails.

If he could   get her   pregnant   then I could   get you   after   the salt. Sap it after   your stitches.

Place the shepherd   the shepherd's purse   under the pestle   along the mortar. There
                    are taste buds   in your throat.   You will   between   changed and   not
                                        the same; you   will taste   the wheel
                                                                with your throat.

It's been days of these Coca-Colas and graham crackers. And I am not after I do not have a son.

I raised   my neck to   the posture   of water   lilies.   Felt the river
                                   pills under   my toes. Looking   for lost
                                                   looking. You   ought too.

My toes never   touched the windshield.   I waited. I   want you   too
know   that.   Your fat   betrays your gender.

You will   not   be asked   to hold your own   chin. This   now, the bottom
               of your foot, will   be your every skin.   Abigail,   honey, here
                                                    circle   that nerve.

I spent the days whacking   out a piano's legs. Hit   the tile like a   jaw. What you call
losing   your virginity   I call every   other   day.

I stayed   in   my office   after it.   Shake the little   Dixie   cups of pearls.
I asked you once   to never   ask after it.

Red petals   on her   eyelids. Been through   my eyelid,   found chowder   all over my   mirror my anything.

For reading, thank you.

For everything, thank you, Dara, Peter, Lisa, Jim, and Jim. Thank you, David, Donna, Haivan, Anne, Daniel, Jenny, Emily, Adam, and Suzanne. Thank you, Kaethe, Jenny, Eliot, Mary, Carol, Tony, and Kathy. Thank you, Ms. Afdahl, Ms. Dockter, Ms. Springer, and Ms. Hoyard. Thank you, Ms. Brennan, Mrs. Bowles, and Mr. Ryan. Teachers help people make it.

Thank you, Emily, Guy, Karl, Jon, and Mary, and everyone at Factory Hollow, for making this.

Thank you, Nat, for *The Motorist* (minutesBOOKS 2010). Thank you, Emily, Shannon, Heather, and everyone at *jubliat*. Thank you, Nick, and Mike, and everyone at *NOO Weekly*.

For your work, thank you, Rae Armantrout, Big Sean, H. D., Peter Gizzi, Kate Greenstreet, Kendrick Lamar, Nathaniel Mackey, Nicki Minaj, Maggie Nelson, Lisa Olstein, Sonia Sanchez, James Schuyler, Christopher Smart, Jack Spicer, Gertrude Stein, James Tate, Rosmarie Waldrop, Dara Wier, and C. D. Wright.

Thank you, Janelle Monáe; for "bibicality," I borrowed a line from "Cold War," *The ArchAndroid*, Bad Boy Records, LLC., 2010.

For being in the writing of this book, and for seeing it though, thank you, Leora Fridman, Sarah Boyer, Nat Otting, Paul Christiansen, Peter Gizzi, Dara Wier, Emily Pettit, David Bartone, Caroline Cabrera, Brett DeFries, Gabe Durham, Madeline Ffitch, Kyle Flak, Brian Foley, Lech Harris, Ben Hersey, Anne Cecelia Holmes, Emily Hunt, Scott Jacobs Jr., Chris Janke, my JIWY workshop, Annie Kleeman-McGurk, Avi Kline, Ben Kopel, Jenny Krichevsky, Kate Litterer, Carrie Lorig, Kate Marantz, Jessica Ouellette, Nate Pritts, Nick Sturm, Matt Suss, Gale Marie Thompson, Jono Tosch, Clay Ventre, Jonathan Volk, Chris Ward, Mike Wall, and Wendy Xu.

For being at *every* reading, and then at the Moan and Dove afterwards, thank you Kate, Elise, and Ashley.

For your support and trust, thank you, Mom, Dad, David, Janet, Dave, Rachel, and Katherine.

For being my first and constant teachers, thank you Mom and Dad.

For all time, I love you, Michael.

Kelin Loe is a founding co-editor of *SPOKE TOO SOON: A Journal of the Longer*. She is the host of Flying Object Radio, and a tour guide at the Emily Dickinson Museum. She received a Masters of Fine Arts from the University of Massachusetts Amherst in 2012, and is currently working towards a PhD in Rhetoric and Composition at the same institution. She lives in Northampton, MA, with her partner, Michael, and their rabbit, Owl.